ISBN Print:  978-1-998651-93-1

Dedicated to Sally

QUEST

I keep seeking out new adventures!
There's a quest inside of me.
Questing day and night
Solving mysteries is my new hobby.

Quests can have very strange histories..
Some are inspirational some are creepy.
I'd like to find the Holy Grail...
But all this questing is making me sleepy!

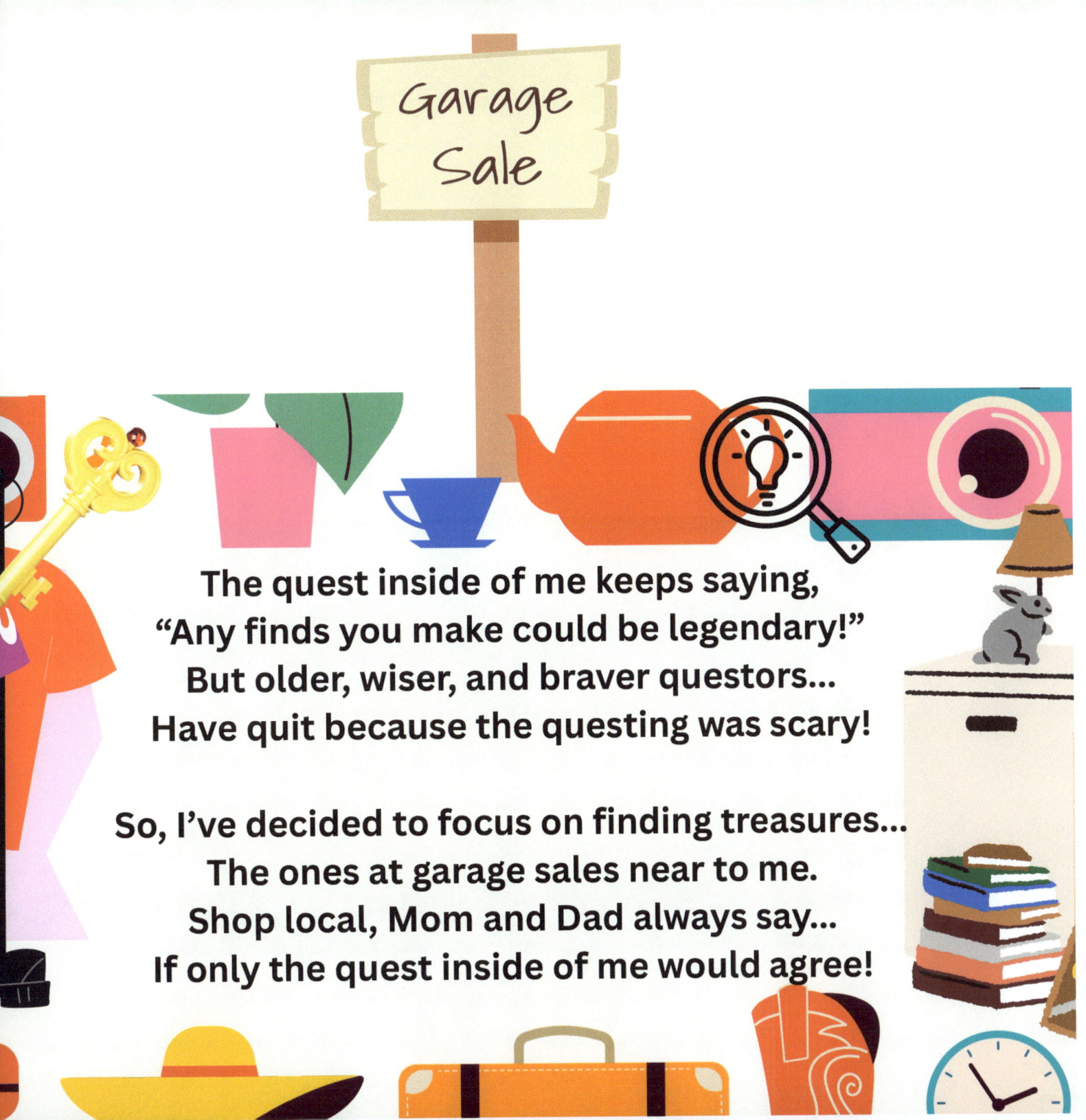

The quest inside of me keeps saying,
"Any finds you make could be legendary!"
But older, wiser, and braver questors...
Have quit because the questing was scary!

So, I've decided to focus on finding treasures...
The ones at garage sales near to me.
Shop local, Mom and Dad always say...
If only the quest inside of me would agree!

VIEW

It can be boring looking out the same window...
Which is why I like to change the view.
Seasons change it, that is true...
But you can do more, when there's a view inside of you.

Close your eyes and lose yourself...
Imagining where you'd like to be!
When you open them up again...
You might even see the VIEW I see!

# CUTTLEFISH

# Cuddle

Sometimes when I feel like a cuddle...
There's a cuttlefish inside of me.
He swims around and around in my tummy...
And the waves he makes cuddle me!

BROOM

I've discovered something weird...
Now that there's a broom inside of me.
I sweep every single inch of my room...
Yes, sweeping relaxes me!

All day long, I sweep, sweep, sweep!
The more sweeping I do, the more energy!
When every inch of the house has been swept...
I go outside and sweep as far as I can see.

Next thing I know, a neighbour comes out.
"Sweeping the street looks like fun!" she says.
"Mind if I join in and sweep with you?" she asks.
We get together and we sweep for days!

Other neighbours see us and join in...
Sweeping for us, is something to behold.
Next thing you know we are in the Curling
League...
Hoping one day sweeping we'll win GOLD!

# GOLDFISH

I woke up with tears in my eyes again...
There's a sadness inside of me.
It started after my goldfish died...
His name was GOLDIE.

When he was no longer alive...
I watched him turn round and round in the drain...
And when he disappeared...
I realised I'd never see my friend again.

I spoke to Goldie, inside my head...
As I imagined him going out into the sea.
Then I understood he would always be...
A living memory inside of me.

# PICKLEBALL

Grandma took me to play pickleball...
And now there's a pickleball inside of me.
Grandma has some moves while playing...
And it was no problem for her to thrash me!

The more competitive she became...
The more I was keen to win!
Pickleball takes skills and is fun...
I like it when she is on my team - we're twins!

Grandma and I, top the granny
and granddaughter league...
My brother and grandpa hope
they'll see...
The day when they can beat us...
It won't happen when there's a
pickleball in me!

CLOUD

If clouds had feet would
they move faster
As they advance across
the sky?
Since there is a cloud in
me...
I might give the feet
thing a try!

ORIGAMI

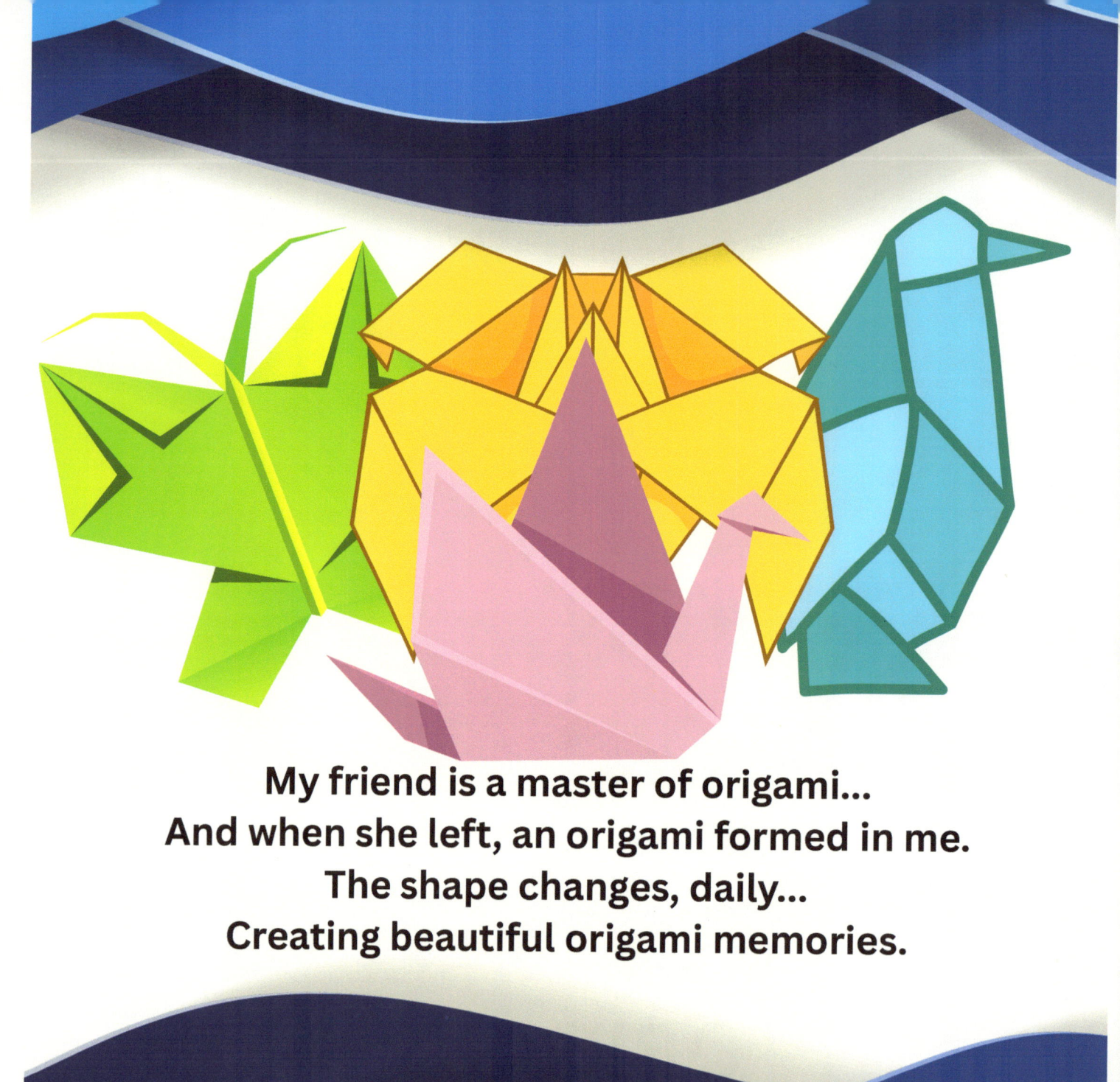

My friend is a master of origami...
And when she left, an origami formed in me.
The shape changes, daily...
Creating beautiful origami memories.

**DIDGERIDOO**

I don't know how to play a didgeridoo!
Even though there's one inside of me.
I'd like to learn if someone in Australia could help!
The lessons on line don't seem to work for me!

# MOCK TURTLE

"Stop mocking me!" I demand.
Of the mock turtle inside of me.
He laughs and rolls over onto his shell...
He says he can't help mocking me!

"It's in my name!" he explains.
His name doesn't matter to me.
"Your name should be RUDE TURTLE!" I
say...
"Because you are always RUDE TO ME!"

The mock turtle inside of me grows quiet...
I can tell he is thinking inside of me...
Then he says, without laughing...
"I think I owe you an apology!"

**HARP**

My life changed the other day...
When a harp played inside of me.
Harps were named after the god of the wind Aeolis...
The harpist's name was Helen, and she played beautifully.

Helen the harpist, never stopped playing...
Even when I asked her questions to distract her.
Such as how many strings were on a harp...
She said forty-seven, but she didn't sound sure.

"Are you an angel?" I asked.
"No," Helen the harpist replied.
"To be an angel," she said,
"I would have had to have died."

That kind of made sense, she kept on playing...
This time it was a lullaby.
Instead of making me want to go to sleep...
Helen the harpist's playing made me cry!

**BOOMERANG**

My dog isn't happy with me anymore...
Not since a boomerang flew inside me.
I don't know who tossed it in the first place...
All I know is the boomerang returned to me.

When I take Roger my dog to the park...
He wants me to throw a ball for him to fetch...
But the only thing I can throw is the boomerang...
And it's a boomerang only I can catch!

So, Roger decided to change the game...
He found a ball and ran away from me!
He ran through the park, and went home...
While I followed, with the boomerang chasing me!

**VAMPIRE SQUID**

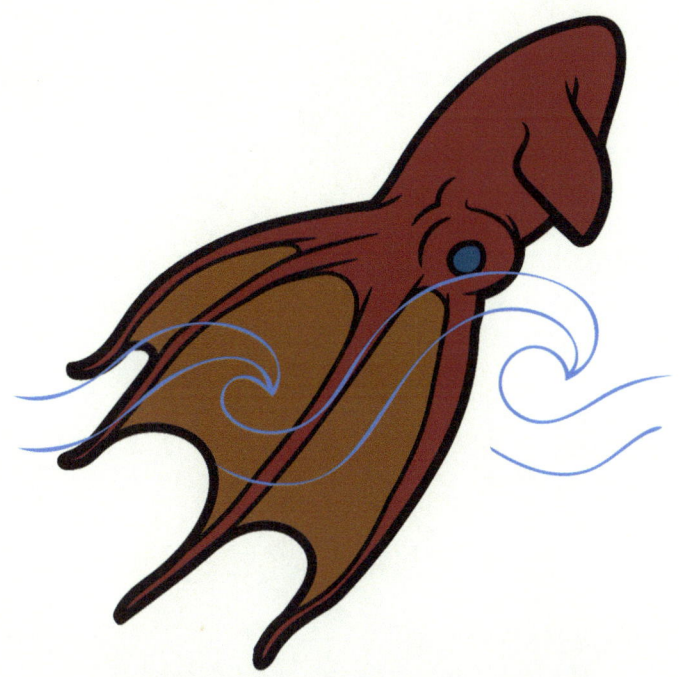

I never heard of a vampire squid before
Until one invaded me.
It is neither a vampire, nor a squid...
And yet it exists, within me.

"Why are you named after things which you are
not?" I inquire.
With its red eyes the vampire stares at me.
"I didn't name myself," it says,
"I don't know why they gave that name to me."

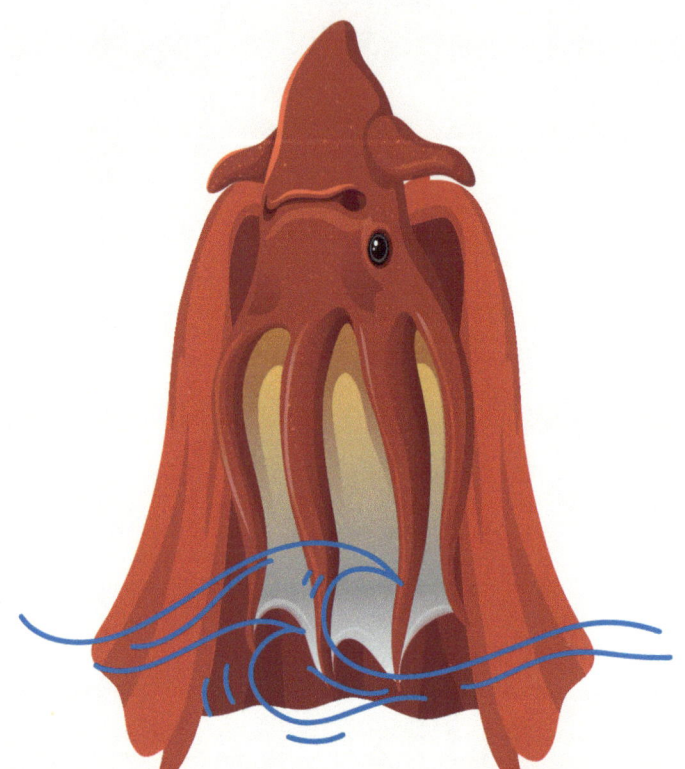

I felt sorry for the poor vampire squid...
Why had someone named him things he was not?
"We have to roll with the punches," he says,
"And focus on the things we are - instead of things we are not.

These wise words were impressive...
And suddenly it occurred to me...
I'm not what my name means either...
My name is Wolf you see!

ARTIST

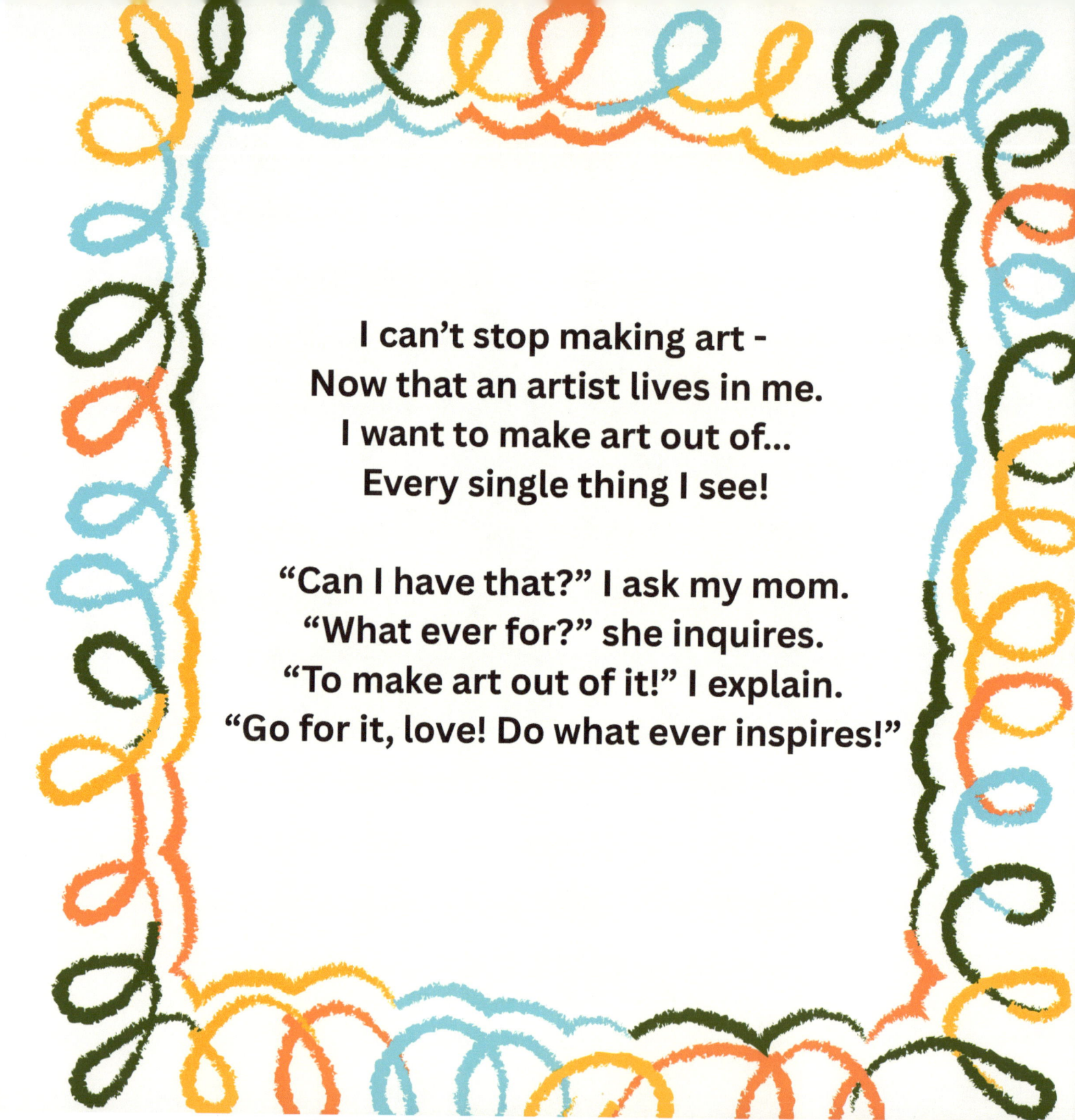

I can't stop making art -
Now that an artist lives in me.
I want to make art out of...
Every single thing I see!

"Can I have that?" I ask my mom.
"What ever for?" she inquires.
"To make art out of it!" I explain.
"Go for it, love! Do what ever inspires!"

I pick up the things, adding others while I go.
Soon, I have a little collection.
I cut, and I paste, I make a collage...
Like all art, it takes a different direction.

I stand back, and view what I've created...
It is good, but it isn't great.
"Come on, let's go and make something else!"
The artist inside me says, "I can't wait!

Now we are going outdoors, carrying canvas and paints...
I'm dressed in my hat like Van Gogh.
We sit near a field of sunflowers...
And we watch the wind as it blows.

The artist inside of me and I are speechless...
We throw paint onto the canvas thick and thin...
Time moves on, and soon it is dark...
I'm not alone. I'm with the artist within.

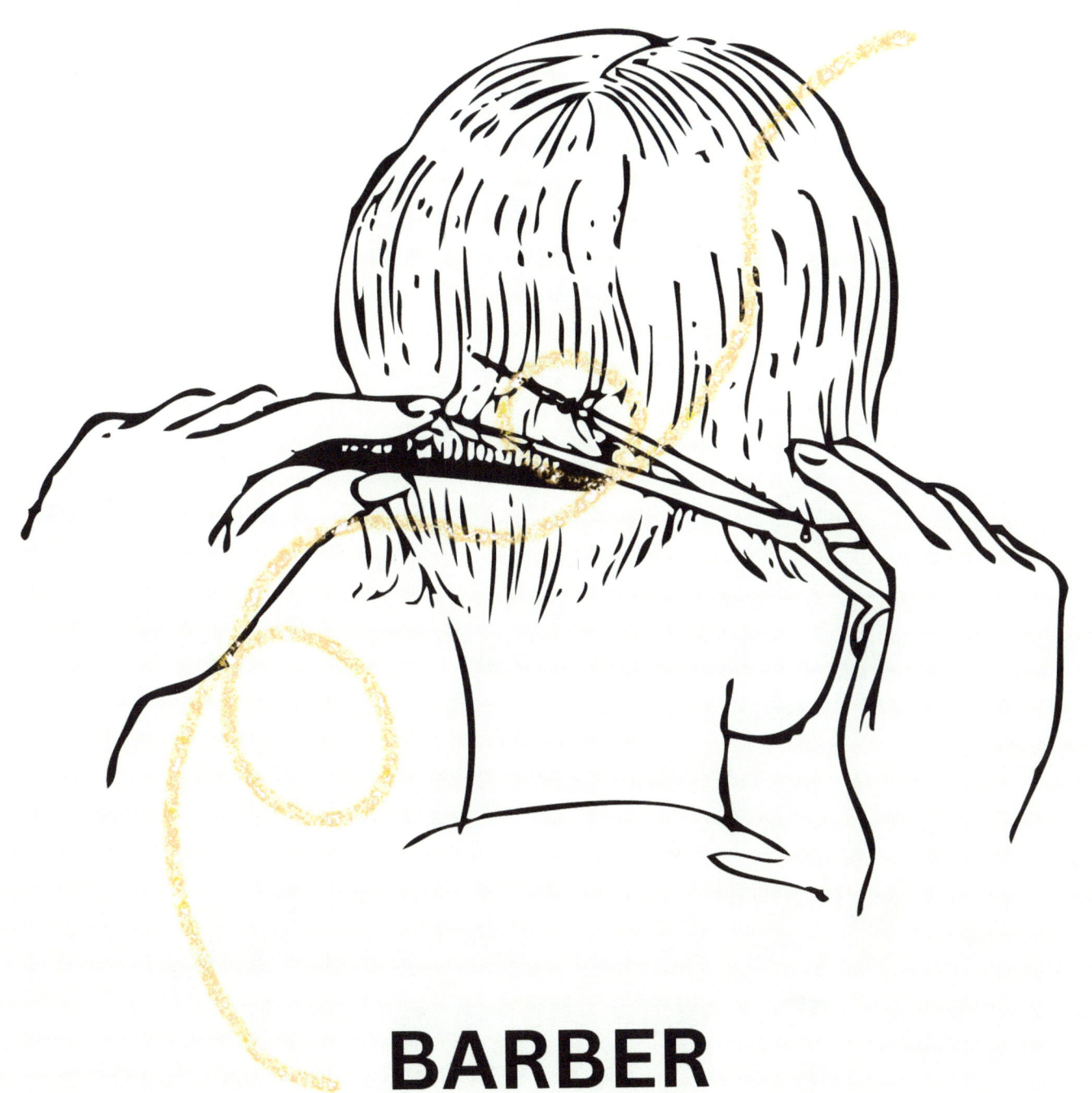

**BARBER**

I know what I want to be when I grow up!
Since a barber moved inside of me.
He said this is one job which won't be taken...
By robots or even I.T.

"People want to be pampered," he said.
"When a barber is cutting their hair.
"Why a robot might cut off an ear!" he said...
"Since they don't have feelings they wouldn't
even care!"

I tell my father; I want to be a barber.
He says, "That's great! Find an apprenticeship then!"
I decide to do something better...
We speak to Dad's barber, a friend called Ken.

Ken asks me why I want to be a barber...
I do an interview, with help from the barber in me.
"You're too young to start working," Ken decides,
"But you're not too young to watch and learn from me."

"You should be paid while you're learning,"
says the barber inside of me.
I find the words to tell Ken...
And he totally agrees with me.

"You'll earn a wage, if your father agrees,"
Ken and my father exchange a glance.
And someday I will open my own Barber Shop...
Thanks to Ken for giving me a chance!

PHOTOGRAPHER

Since my Mom and Dad gave me
my first phone,
There's a photographer living
inside of me.
Click, click, click, goes that
camera...
I zoom it, and love the art of
photography.

Somethings are easy to
photograph...
Because they remain still...
Others by the time I point and
click...
Move about at will.

It seems to me that every day life...
Is a little like the art of photography...
One never knows what will happen from day to day...
Or what amazing sights we will see.

I can master different photos...
Thanks to the photographer inside of me...
But as of yet, I haven't been able to...
Learn how to take a decent selfie!

# selfie ♥

DOCTOR

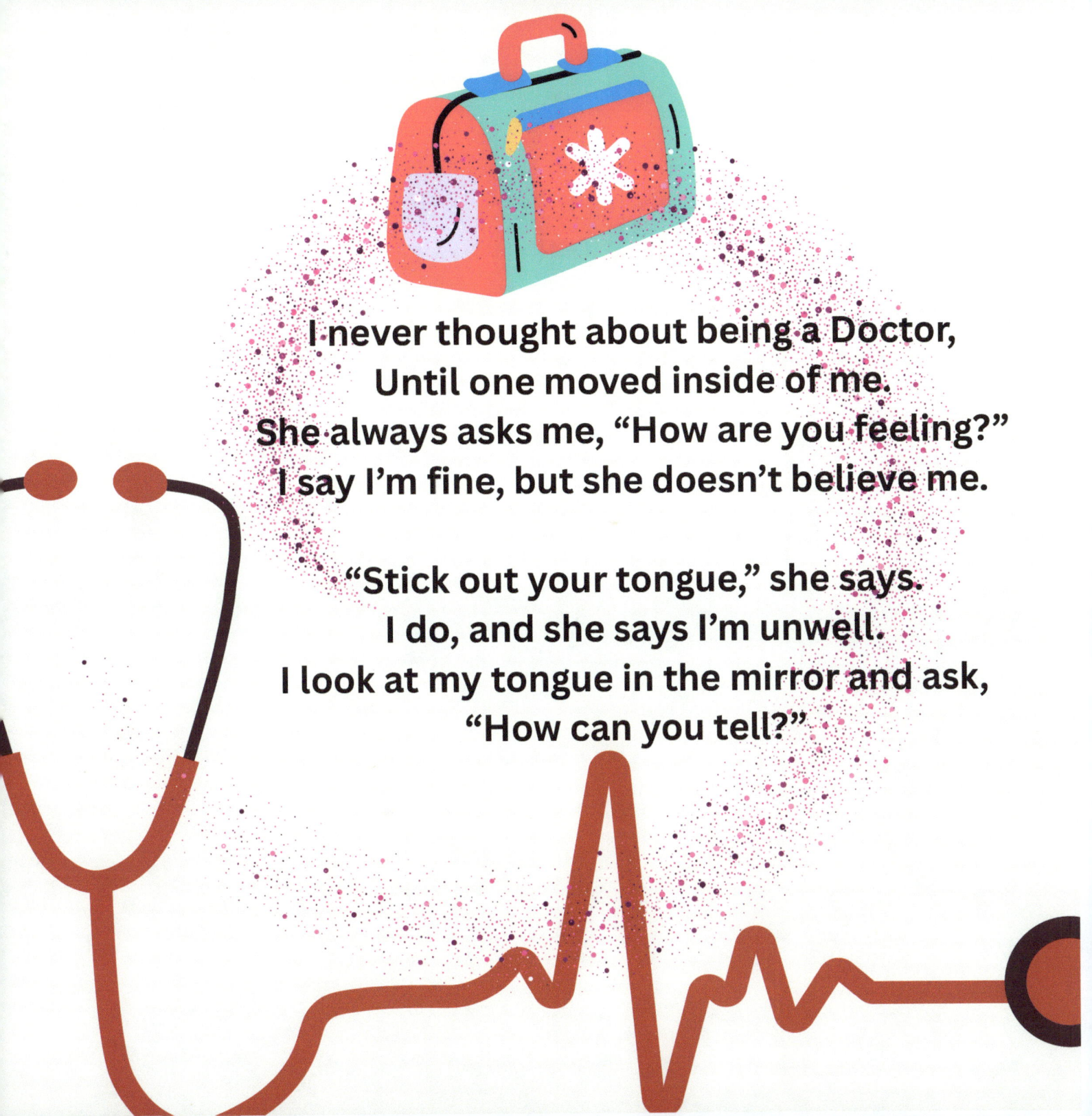

I never thought about being a Doctor,
Until one moved inside of me.
She always asks me, "How are you feeling?"
I say I'm fine, but she doesn't believe me.

"Stick out your tongue," she says.
I do, and she says I'm unwell.
I look at my tongue in the mirror and ask,
"How can you tell?"

"I'm a Doctor," she says, and it's
my job to know.
"Now back into bed you go!"
Mom and Dad come in, they feel
my forehead...
If I'm sick or not they don't know.

The Doctor inside of me pipes in...
"Tell them to look at your tongue!"
she says to me.
I do, but they don't see
symptoms...
Which is why I want to be a Doctor
you see!

GNOME

I used to love to sit in our back garden...
Before the gnome moved inside of me.
Then, when I sat in the garden...
He was nestled among the trees.

But now that he lives inside me...
All he does is complain...
He misses the sunshine...
And he even misses the rain!

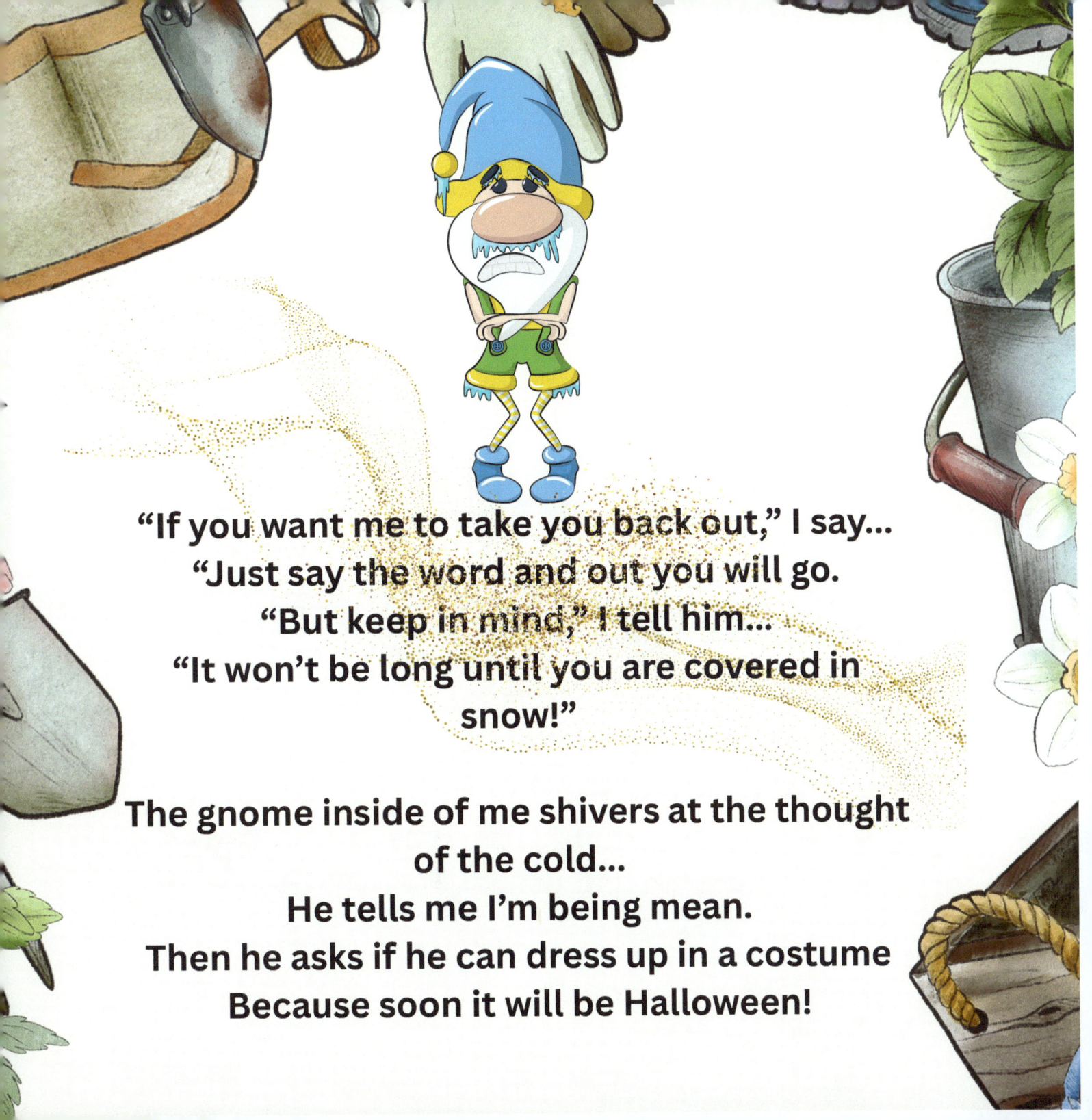

"If you want me to take you back out," I say...
"Just say the word and out you will go.
"But keep in mind," I tell him...
"It won't be long until you are covered in snow!"

The gnome inside of me shivers at the thought of the cold...
He tells me I'm being mean.
Then he asks if he can dress up in a costume
Because soon it will be Halloween!

We come to an agreement...
Myself and the gnome inside of me.
In spring and summer, he lives in the garden...
In autumn and winter, he lives in me.

# ALSO BY CATHY MCGOUGH

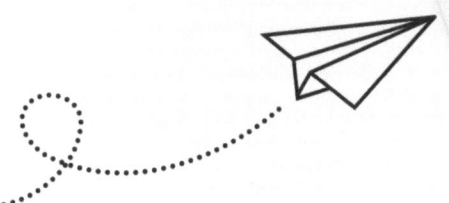